BUFFALO GAL

A R Gurney

BROADWAY PLAY PUBLISHING INC
56 E 81st St., NY NY 10028-0202
212 772-8334 fax: 212 772-8358
http://www.BroadwayPlayPubl.com

Say When was written by Thomas Cabaniss, with lyrics
by A R Gurney. The sheet music is available for
licensed stage productions. The song credits must
appear in all production programs.

An earlier version of this play was published in
September 2002.

First printing: December 2008
I S B N: 0-88145-428-1

Word processing: Microsoft Word for Windows
Typographic controls: Xerox Ventura Publisher 2.0 P E
Typeface: Palatino
Printed on recycled acid-free paper and bound in the
U S A

ABOUT THE AUTHOR

A R Gurney has written many plays. Among them are: THE DINING ROOM, THE COCKTAIL HOUR, LOVE LETTERS, SYLVIA, FAR EAST, and INDIAN BLOOD. He has also written several novels, a few television scripts, and the libretto of a one-act opera. He has received a number of awards including ones from the Drama Desk, the National Endowment of the Arts, the Rockefeller Foundation. He is a member of The American Academy of Arts and Letters, of the Theater Hall of Fame, and a Lucille Lortel Award winner for the body of his work. He has honorary degrees from Williams College and Buffalo State College S U N Y. He taught literature at M I T for many years before committing himself to full-time writing.

BUFFALO GAL was first produced at the
Williamstown Theater Festival (Michael Ritchie,
producer) on 13 June 2000. The cast and creative
contributors were as follows:

AMANDA . . . . .Mariette Hartley
JACKIE . . . . Becky Ann Baker
ROY . . . . Michael Mastro
DEBBIE . . . . .Michi Barall
JAMES . . . . Peter Francis James
DAN . . . . .Michael Gross

Director . . . . John Tillinger
Set design . . . . Jim Noone
Lighting design . . . . Kevin Adams
Costume design . . . . Laurie Churba
Stage manager . . . . .Barclay Stiff

The play then opened for a regular run at the Studio Arena Theater in Buffalo, NY (Gavin Cameron-Webb, artistic director) on 21 March 2002, with the following cast and creative contributors:

AMANDA . . . . Betty Buckley
JACKIE . . . . Mary Beth Fisher
ROY . . . . Eddie Korbich
DEBBIE . . . . Aiko Nakasone
JAMES . . . . Jonathan Earl Peck
DAN . . . . Julian Gamble

Director . . . . John Tillinger
Lighting design . . . . Jim Vermeulen
Stage manager . . . . Nanci Sochol

A revised version of BUFFALO GAL was produced in New York City by Primary Stages (Casey Childs, Executive Producer; Andrew Leynse, Artistic Director; Elliot Fox, Managing Director) in association with Jamie de Roy and Alan D Marks, with its first public performance on 22 July 2008. The cast and creative contributors were as follows:

AMANDA .... Susan Sullivan
JACKIE .... Jennifer Regan
ROY .... James Waterston
DEBBIE .... Carmen M Herlihy
JAMES ....Dathan B Williams
DAN .... Mark Blum

Director .... Mark Lamos
Set design .... Andrew Jackness
Costume design .... Candice Donnelly
Lighting design ....Mary Louise Geiger
Original music & sound design .... John Gromada
Production stage manager .... Matthew Melchiorre
Production supervisor .... P R F Productions
Casting ....Stephanie Klapper Casting
Press Representative .... O & M Co
Director of marketing ....Shanta Mali
Associate artistic director .... Michelle Bossy

to John Tillinger and Mark Lamos,
with continued appreciation

CHARACTERS & SETTING

ROY
DEBBIE, *younger*
JACKIE
AMANDA
JAMES
DAN

Buffalo, NY

Time: Today

Set: The stage of a regional theater in Buffalo, New York. The play takes place on a Monday afternoon, before the Tuesday when rehearsals are to begin for Chekhov's **The Cherry Orchard**. *Since this will be the first production of the season, the company has the luxury of using the stage. A pile of lighting instruments, yet to be hung, is visible. A prop table is in evidence, with various makeshift props. Some of the stage floor has been marked off with bright colored tape, to indicate the ground plans for the various acts. Pieces of tacky rehearsal furniture are placed around, to be moved as necessary. Off to one side might be the usual rehearsal coffee maker with a few chipped cups. Somewhere else on stage is a work table with chairs for the director and stage manager.*

Time: Today

Before rise: A lively choral version of the old song:

Buffalo gals, won't you come out tonight,
come out tonight,
come out tonight,
Buffalo gals, won't you come out tonight,
And dance by the light of the moon...

(At rise:)

(ROY, the production stage manager, is checking the outlines of the set, already indicated by strips of brightly colored adhesive tape. He works carefully, consulting a large copy of the designer's ground plan on the floor. DEBBIE, his young assistant stage manager, works with him, holding a spool tape measure.)

ROY: *(Checking plans with a ruler)* Fourteen feet...

(They measure a taped line on stage.)

DEBBIE: *(Reading the tape measure)* Fourteen feet...

(ROY lets go of his end of the tape measure. It snaps to DEBBIE, who jumps.)

ROY: Now, to the window...let's see... *(Checking plans)* Ten feet seven inches.

(They measure.)

DEBBIE: *(Reading)* Ten seven. More or less.

ROY: Which is it?

DEBBIE: What?

ROY: Is it more or is it less?

DEBBIE: *(Checking)* Ten feet five and one half inches.

ROY: That's less.

DEBBIE: Isn't it close enough?

ROY: No. We'll have to fix it later.

(The tape measure snaps closed again.)

(JACKIE *comes out from the wings. She is the director of the theater, wearing efficient clothes, toting a work bag.*)

JACKIE: She's here.

ROY: (*Stopping work*) At her hotel?

JACKIE: (*Indicating offstage*) No, here! In the theater. Checking out her dressing room.

ROY: Total!

(ROY *and* JACKIE *give each other a triumphant high five.*)

ROY: Did she like the flowers?

JACKIE: She did.

ROY: One dozen roses. With a card saying, "Welcome home".

JACKIE: And the basket of fruit from the Board members.

DEBBIE: What did she say?

JACKIE: She said "Whom do I thank for these goodies?"

ROY: "Whom"? She said, "Whom"?

JACKIE: And when I told her they came from the theater, she said, "Thank you, theater!" and gave this big swooping bow. (*She imitates it.*)

DEBBIE: Is she glad to be back in Buffalo?

JACKIE: "Thrilled!" She said. "Thrilled."

DEBBIE: Do you think she'd like a Buffalo Bills T-shirt?

JACKIE: (*Dryly*) Not immediately.

ROY: How does she look?

JACKIE: Gorgeous and glamorous. But she wants us to change her hotel.

ROY: The Hyatt isn't good enough?

JACKIE: She wants to stay with the other actors.

ROY: At the *Lenox*?

JACKIE: That's what she said.

ROY: The Lenox is definitely not the Hyatt.

JACKIE: I told her that, but that's what she wants.

DEBBIE: The Lenox used to be one of the most elegant hotels in Buffalo.

ROY: The Lenox?

DEBBIE: I read it in a book. It has Tiffany glass windows in the lobby.

ROY: But it is not the Hyatt. *(To* JACKIE*)* We should make sure they give her their best room.

JACKIE: Right.

*(*ROY *makes a note)*

JACKIE: She doesn't even want a car.

ROY: What?

JACKIE: I told her we'd rent her a car, but no. She wants to ride in the van with the rest of the cast.

DEBBIE: She sounds very democratic.

JACKIE: That's one way to look at it, Debbie.

DEBBIE: She was on T V last night.

ROY: Saw it. Re-run of *C S I—Miami.*

DEBBIE: She was wonderful.

ROY: She played a judge with Alzheimer's.

JACKIE: Sounds challenging.

ROY: She pulled it off.

DEBBIE: I read somewhere she's great to work with.

JACKIE: That always helps.

ROY: I hear she likes to improvise.

JACKIE: That usually doesn't.

ROY: What's the problem, Jackie.

JACKIE: No problem.

ROY: Come on. We've worked together on—what?
—This will be our seventh production. I can tell
something's eating you.

JACKIE: She's scared.

DEBBIE: Of what?

JACKIE: This. Us. The whole thing.

ROY: Returning to the stage?

JACKIE: She shows up a day early because she needs
a "head start", quote unquote. Then this Lenox thing.
And riding in the van...

DEBBIE: Maybe she wants to feel part of the company.

JACKIE: Maybe she wants to hide behind the other
actors.

ROY: Sometimes it's hard to come home.

DEBBIE: That is so true. Every time I go home, I regress.
And my parents live right here in Buffalo.

JACKIE: She made me give her a tour of the city on the
way in from the airport.

DEBBIE: That means she cares.

JACKIE: Oh she cares. You could say she cares
desperately.

ROY: Did you tell her we've lost Marty Carr?

JACKIE: (Looking off) Ssshh. Not yet... Did the mail come?

ROY: It did.

JACKIE: Any sign of her contract?

ROY: They'll probably Fed-Ex it.

JACKIE: Yeah, but when?

DEBBIE: She wants to do the play, doesn't she?

JACKIE: She keeps saying she does.

DEBBIE: In that interview she said she was thrilled.

JACKIE: There you go: *(Imitating her)* "Thrilled." Also, "Delighted" ...And "frantic to come back..."

ROY: And she's here.

JACKIE: What did Juliet say last spring? "I have a faint cold fear..."

DEBBIE: *(Acting it)*
"I have a faint cold fear thrills through my veins
That almost freezes up the heat of life ..."

JACKIE: Not bad, Debbie.

DEBBIE: I was Juliet's dresser last spring, remember? I heard that speech every night.

JACKIE: You may hear it again. From me.

AMANDA: *(Calling from offstage)* Hello!

JACKIE: Hark, hark, the lark. *(Calling toward off)* We're out here! On stage!

(A moment. Then AMANDA makes an entrance. She is middle-aged, beautiful, and a star.)

AMANDA: Nobody say a word for one brief minute. *(Finally:)* This is it, isn't it?

JACKIE: This is what?

AMANDA: It! This! *(Stamping her foot on the stage; the others jump)* The stage! Two boards and a passion! This is what I've been missing. *(Walks around)* Oh my heavens, it's hard to believe. I am actually back on stage! Who was that Greek hero who regained his

strength whenever his feet touched the ground?
Anyone know?

DEBBIE: Antaeus.

AMANDA: Antaeus!

JACKIE: Debbie's our scholar in residence.

AMANDA: Thank you, Debbie! I feel like Antaeus.
I can almost feel my strength returning, now I'm back
on stage.

JACKIE: And back home, too.

AMANDA: Home! Remember what F Scott Fitzgerald
said about home? ...Let's see.... *(She tries to remember.)*
And he lived in Buffalo, too.

DEBBIE: He did.

AMANDA: I should definitely know this...
"Americans—" Now wait. I'm terrible with lines...

(The others glance anxiously at each other.)

AMANDA: He said "Americans always want to be back
somewhere." Something like that, only he said it better.

ROY: Welcome home, anyway.

JACKIE: This is Roy, our stage manager ...

AMANDA: Roy ... *(Shaking hands)* How do you do, Roy...

ROY: A pleasure, Miss—

AMANDA: *(Interrupting)* First names only, please. I want
everyone to call me Amanda.

ROY: O K, Amanda.

JACKIE: Debbie is our A S M.

AMANDA: A S M...A S M...

JACKIE: Assistant Stage Manager...

AMANDA: Of course! Forgive me, Debbie. The motor's still there, the battery just needs recharging. *(Kisses* DEBBIE)

JACKIE: Debbie's a theater major out at the university. She's interning with us, learning the practical side.

DEBBIE: I'm trying to decide whether to make it my career.

AMANDA: Do it, Debbie, do it! I wish I had.

ROY: You did.

AMANDA: I did not, Roy. I let myself be hijacked by Hollywood. But now I'm doing Chekhov, my absolute favorite playwright, and I'm thrilled! *(Taking a bow)* Anton Chekhov, I'll try to do well by you!

DEBBIE: Did you have a nice trip, Amanda?

AMANDA: I'll say this, Debbie dear: it's a long way from Hollywood to Buffalo.

ROY: You have to change in Chicago.

AMANDA: Yes you do, Roy. You definitely have to change. And I believe I did. As we were driving in from the airport, I finally felt like a Buffalo gal again. My whole past life came surging back around me! I said to Jackie here, "Get me off this stupid Freeway! Take me the long way around!"

JACKIE: *(To others)* We came in Main Street.

AMANDA: And turned down Amherst and zipped by the zoo. Which looks exactly the same: those sad old bison, standing around munching hay. And then we ducked into the Park, where, I admit, I saw a major adjustment.

ROY: What was that?

AMANDA: The statue of David. He's not wearing a fig leaf now! Things must be loosening up at last!

JACKIE: In some areas.

AMANDA: In some important areas, I might add....
Oh, and then we swept down Delaware Avenue,
which is surely one of the great thoroughfares of the
Western World! The elms may be gone, but those
lovely old houses linger on!

ROY: Mostly charitable organizations now.

AMANDA: But they're there, Roy! They're still there!
I made Jackie turn down Summer Street, to see if my
Grandmother's house was there, too.

JACKIE: Which it was.

AMANDA: With guess what? A For Sale sign right on
the front lawn.

JACKIE: *(To* ROY*)* How about that? We're doing *The
Cherry Orchard*, and the family domicile is up for sale.

DEBBIE: Life imitates art!

JACKIE: May we quote you on that, Debbie?

AMANDA: I'm sure it's been bought and sold many
times since my grandmother died.

JACKIE: *(To* ROY *and* DEBBIE*)* One of those solid old jobs,
with a large porch across the front.

AMANDA: Veranda. My grandmother called it the
veranda. I'd stay with her when my parents were away,
and she'd say, "Let's go out on the veranda, Amanda.
Let's view the passing parade." *(Tearfully)* Then she'd
put on her gloves—she was always putting on her
gloves—and we'd settle into these wicker rockers,
and wave at people passing by. She knew everybody.
Or I should say everybody knew her. A veranda is a
wonderful thing.

DEBBIE: Buffalo is famous for its architecture. We have
five houses by Frank Lloyd Wright.

AMANDA: I know that, Debbie, dear. Of course, my grandmother's house looks like a boarding house now. *(Sadly)* Times change, times change. *(She is momentarily lost in thought.)*

JACKIE: *(Brightly)* We got out and looked around.

AMANDA: We did. And listen to this, you two. There's still the old barn in back, which became the garage. We peeked in a window. And even the tack room is still there. With the cot where the chauffeur slept. And there's still the old turn-table, though I doubt if it still works.

ROY: Turn-table?

AMANDA: For carriages. And then cars. My grandmother had this old Pierce Arrow, made right here in Buffalo. The turn-table was so the chauffer could simply turn the car around and drive it out front first. My grandmother thought it was vulgar ever to back up.

JACKIE: It must have been tough to parallel park.

AMANDA: I'm sure it was. But that turntable was important to her. "Never back out of anything," she'd say. "Whatever you do, go forward." Oh I loved my grandmother. And she loved me. I was her favorite.

ROY: Any family still here, Amanda?

AMANDA: No. Oh, there used to be lots of us. We were positively Tolstoyan. I mean, all four of my *grand*parents were *born* here. But they've long since gone, of course. And my parents have gone. And the rest have moved away. *(To* JACKIE*)* Isn't that what people do in Buffalo these days? They go.

JACKIE: Some come back..

ROY: Jackie came back from the west coast.

JACKIE: *(To* AMANDA*)* From my Equity-waver theater in West Hollywood.

AMANDA: Which I remember well. Your production of *Streetcar* made me want to work with you.

ROY: Jackie devoted her last season in L A to the early plays of Eugene O'Neill.

AMANDA: I know, I know. I saw her *Strange Interlude.* Or most of it.

JACKIE: Thank God for the interludes, right?

AMANDA: I had an early call the next day

ROY: Jackie won a directing award for that.

JACKIE: Big deal. We were ultimately a burp in the belly of the film industry. I can do more here.

AMANDA: So can I! This is so...three-dimensional. Maybe it's the breeze off Lake Erie. Or maybe it's just my genes. My grandmother used to say, "Go where you like, Amanda. Do what you want. But you'll always be a Buffalo gal at heart." You must feel that way, too, Jackie.

JACKIE: Sometimes.

AMANDA: Because it's home, isn't it? Home. Even with my family gone, and my grandmother's house in rack and ruin, it's still home, which is one of the sweetest words in the English language.

(Another emotional moment)

JACKIE: Could we talk about the play?

AMANDA: Oh yes. Absolutely. What a lovely space.

JACKIE: Luckily this is our first show this season, so we can rehearse on stage.

ROY: At least till they start putting in the rest of the set.

JACKIE: We wanted to make things easier for you, Amanda. These tapes will give you some idea of the ground plan.

ROY: *(Indicating)* That line there should extend an inch and a half longer, to meet that diagonal from a window seat.

AMANDA: *(Vaguely)* I see.

JACKIE: We'll show you the model.

ROY: Debbie...

JACKIE: It's in my office.

ROY: Be careful with it.

(DEBBIE hurries off)

ROY: Oh. Hey. Amanda. While we're waiting.... *(Taking a pink slip off his clipboard)* Ginny picked up a phone message for you. From some Doctor. *(Hands the slip to her)*

AMANDA: Doctor? *(Putting on her glasses)* Doctor who? *(Tries to read)*

ROY: Ginny's writing leaves something to be desired. *(Reading over her shoulder)* I believe that says "Doctor Robbins".

AMANDA: Never heard of him.

ROY: He says, "When can I see you."

AMANDA: About what?

JACKIE: I hope you're not sick.

AMANDA: Not that I know of.

JACKIE: Probably some fan.

AMANDA: Maybe I should call back.

JACKIE: I wouldn't.

AMANDA: I mean, a doctor ...

JACKIE: Might be some crank.

ROY: *(Starting out)* I'll check him out.

AMANDA: Be tactful. No point in losing a fan.

JACKIE: Or a subscriber.

ROY: Right.

AMANDA: If he's a psychiatrist, ask for an appointment. Say I've got a bad case of stage fright.

JACKIE: Oh stop.

(ROY goes)

AMANDA: *(To* JACKIE*)* He's a good stage manager.

JACKIE: The best. He turned down a lucrative tour to work with you.

ROY: *(From off)* I also wanted to work with you, Jackie.

(DEBBIE returns with the model of the set.)

DEBBIE: Here we are. *(Puts it on a table)*

AMANDA: Oh how lovely.

JACKIE: It will help orient you. The designer is fresh from studying with Ming Cho Lee at Yale.

AMANDA: *(Dramatically) The Cherry Orchard* by Anton Chekhov. *(Looking)* And of course this is Act One. The nursery.

JACKIE: *(Indicating)* Door to the outside. Door to your daughter's room. And window looking out on the cherry orchard.

DEBBIE: *(Indicating a taped area)* See? Here's the window.

AMANDA: *(Quoting Chekhov)* "The nursery! My sweet, wonderful room! ...And here I am, back in my own childhood! And... And..." *(Pause)* Oh Lord, I forget what comes next.

JACKIE: That's all right.

AMANDA: It's not all right. Nancy Marchand—who came from Buffalo—once told me that you should memorize your whole part ahead of time, so you could concentrate on the feelings. I was sure I had nailed down Act I.

DEBBIE: Would you like me to get on book? I mean, just to help you along. *(She picks up the script)*

AMANDA: Would you, Debbie? I've been practicing on my stair-master. But that's hardly the stage.

DEBBIE: I'll try to keep you on track.

AMANDA: Good. And be ruthless. I want to get it right, even if you have to follow me around, barking lines like a drill sergeant.

JACKIE: Take it easy.

AMANDA: No, but in the movies or television, lines are a cinch. They give you these little chunks of dialogue, one day at a time. You glance at them before you go on camera, and forget them immediately after. And you don't have to be letter perfect either. You just try to make it sound right. Half the time, what comes out is better than what they wrote.

JACKIE: Sometimes.

AMANDA: But here. On stage. With Chekhov. It should be flawless. I'm shaking in my boots. You'll have to ply me with Prozac, Debbie. I'm serious.

JACKIE: Now, now...

AMANDA: Oh, I'm just being melodramatic. The lines will come. Because this part is me, isn't it? It's in my genes.

(ROY *returns, with another pink slip of paper.*)

ROY: I got his office. Turns out he's a dentist.

AMANDA: Good Lord. Is there something wrong with my teeth?

ROY: (*Reading from slip*) His name is Robbins now, but it was originally Rubin. Daniel Rubin.

AMANDA: Danny Rubin?

JACKIE: Ring a bell?

AMANDA: Oh it does, it does.

ROY: He got on the line.

AMANDA: He did?

ROY: He said he thought you knew he had changed his name.

AMANDA: (*Taking the slip*) I do now.

ROY: He wants to see you.

AMANDA: Oh dear.

JACKIE: You don't want to see him?

AMANDA: I don't know.

(AMANDA *returns the slip to* ROY.)

ROY: Here are his numbers. (*Hands her the pink slip*) Office. And cell..

AMANDA: Oh boy.

JACKIE: You don't have to do anything about it, you know.

AMANDA: I don't know if I can. (*Returns the slip*)

JACKIE: Then don't.

AMANDA: (*Takes the slip again*) Maybe I should.

JACKIE: You've got four weeks of rehearsal, and three weeks of performances to make up your mind. So let's move on.

AMANDA: Yes. Exactly. Work. "We must work", as Chekhov says. *(Returns the slip to* ROY*)*

JACKIE: *(At the model)* Now here...

ROY: Careful. *(Taking over)* I'll do it.

JACKIE: Act Two of *The Cherry Orchard*. Where we move out of doors. See? The nursery become...this.

*(*ROY *adjusts the model.)*

AMANDA: Oh lovely... Do I sit on that little bench?

JACKIE: If you want.

AMANDA: I think I should. *(She finds something to sit on)* I'll sit and say... *(She gets ready)* What do I say?...

ROY: *(Quickly)* Debbie...

*(*DEBBIE *tries to find the place in the script.)*

AMANDA: *(Reaching for it)* "Oh my sins! I've spent my money recklessly, like an insane woman. And married a man who spent even more..." Is that right, Debbie? Is that remotely what I say?

DEBBIE: I'm checking. *(She frantically searches.)*

AMANDA: "My husband drank himself to death" —now stop me if I'm wrong, Debbie— "and then, worst luck, I fell in love with somebody else, and lived with him. And then..." —are you with me, Debbie? Am I close?

DEBBIE: *(Finding it)* Pretty close. *(Shakes her head furtively to the others)*

AMANDA: Oh I hate this next part, when she talks about losing her son. It reminds me of my daughter. I have this daughter, and I'm afraid she's... *(Pause)* Of course, that's my problem, isn't it? I don't intend to foist it on everyone else.

JACKIE: Let's change to Act Three. The drawing room, where they have the party.

AMANDA: Good idea! Yes! The party when they sell the cherry orchard. And where she says...where she says...

(AMANDA *looks to* DEBBIE *for help;* DEBBIE *is frantically trying to find the place in the script.*)

AMANDA: "I was born here, my father and mother lived here, and my grandmother as well."

DEBBIE: *(Checking the script)* Grand*father*...

AMANDA: I know. I was just improvising.

(JACKIE *glances at the others*)

AMANDA: "Without the cherry orchard, my life is meaningless. If you have to sell it, sell me, too!"

ROY: That's great!

DEBBIE: *(Reading from script)* Actually it's..."If it really must be sold, then sell me with the orchard."

AMANDA: See what I do? I paraphrase. The curse of Hollywood.

JACKIE: The feelings were there.

AMANDA: "If it really must be sold, then sell me with the orchard." ... Oh boy. I know what that means, all right, all right.

JACKIE: Hold it. I just had a brainstorm.

AMANDA: About what?

JACKIE: The poster. And the cover of the program. And the newspaper ads. Have we got time to change all that, Roy?

ROY: I'll text Alice....

JACKIE: What if we had a picture of Amanda in front of her grandmother's house, with the For Sale sign and everything?

AMANDA: Oh I don't know.

JACKIE: It would say everything. You. The world of Chekhov. The world of Buffalo. Both going to seed, both looking for ways to face the future.

AMANDA: Of course! That's so true! That's exactly why I'm doing this play! But my grandmother's house is hardly a country estate.

JACKIE: We'd just show a corner of it—part of the veranda, maybe, and a glimpse of the barn. Enough to suggest there could be a cherry orchard in back.

AMANDA: There was an apple tree, I remember.

JACKIE: There you are!

ROY: *(Checking the schedule on his clipboard)* Let's see. To make the printer's Wednesday deadline, we'd have to do it today. And we probably should do Amanda and the house separately, to get the best of both. The graphics people can combine them on the computer.

JACKIE: Get on the phone to Billy.

ROY: Uh-oh. Billy's in Toronto, doing photos for *Hairspray,*

JACKIE: Shit.

ROY: But hey, I could do Amanda myself, and Billy could do the house tomorrow....

JACKIE: Yes? *(To* AMANDA*)* Roy takes head shots on the side.

AMANDA: *(Unenthusiastically)* How...enterprising. And what would I possibly wear?

ROY: Tania in costumes could pull several pieces from stock..

AMANDA: I'd need a wig.

ROY: *(To* JACKIE*)* We held onto that one from *Long Day's Journey.*

AMANDA: Sounds a little tired. *(To* JACKIE*)* I suppose, in a pinch, I could do my own hair. If I have veto power over the results.

JACKIE: Of course.

ROY: *(Making notes)* I'll send Scotty home for my stuff, and see where Tania is on the costume, and call Kenny about the lights..

JACKIE: Say we want an autumnal look...a fading city... a fading world...

(ROY hurries off.)

AMANDA: *(Calling after him)* And a fading me!

JACKIE: Stop that now. *(Returning to the model)* Let's look at Act Four. This slides out here, and this comes in here, and lo and behold! Back to the nursery in Act One. Except there are no curtains on the windows now. And all the furniture is piled up in the corner.

AMANDA: "My life, my youth, my happiness, goodbye!"

DEBBIE: *(Checking script)* Good!

AMANDA: Oh I know this lady. She's in my bones. *(Gaining confidence)* "One last look at these walls, these windows... Oh my mother loved this room..."

DEBBIE: *(Reading)* "...mother used to walk around this room..."

JACKIE: *(To* AMANDA*)* I think Chekhov wants you to walk.

AMANDA: Of course he does! "Walk..." That helps, to walk around. Like this. *(She demonstrates.)*

JACKIE: Great.

AMANDA: Oh I hope, I hope...

JACKIE: Anyway that's the set.

AMANDA: Tell the designer I adore it. I want to sleep with him immediately.

JACKIE: Fat chance.

DEBBIE: You could try. He's flying up tomorrow for the meet-and-greet.

AMANDA: Meet and greet? Oh my God, the other actors! Where are they hiding? Probably off at the Anchor Bar, eating Buffalo wings and whispering how terrible I'll be.

JACKIE: They arrive tomorrow, too, Amanda. Remember? You asked for this extra day..

AMANDA: Oh right.

JACKIE: Actually there is one actor in town already.

AMANDA: Who?

JACKIE: James Johnson. He's taking over for Marty Carr.

AMANDA: Where's Marty?

JACKIE: He dropped out Saturday.

AMANDA: What?

JACKIE: He got a cushy airlines commercial in Kuala Lumpur.

AMANDA: You might have told me, Jackie.

JACKIE: I didn't dare.

AMANDA: I can see why. This upsets me very much.

JACKIE: I apologize.

AMANDA: Marty's a friend. I did a movie with him.
I was looking forward to working with him again.

JACKIE: You'll like James.

AMANDA: He's local?

JACKIE: In a way, yes.

AMANDA: In what way? Is he Equity?

JACKIE: Of course.

AMANDA: I'll need all the help I can get , Jackie.

JACKIE: You'll get it from James.

AMANDA: Maybe I should meet him.

JACKIE: You will, tomorrow.

AMANDA: No I mean now.

JACKIE: You want him to audition?

AMANDA: We certainly should meet....

JACKIE: He'll see it as an audition, Amanda.

AMANDA: Well I'm sorry. I hate to be a stickler on this,
Jackie, but if I don't like him, I might ask you to get
someone else.

JACKIE: Tell Roy to call James, Debbie. Say Amanda
would like to meet him.

DEBBIE: Today?

AMANDA: As soon as possible.

DEBBIE: O K. (Starts out)

AMANDA: Am I being bitchy, Debbie?

DEBBIE: No.

AMANDA: I have to be. A bad actor makes everyone
else look bad. Especially in the theater. In the movies or
television, the director can fix it up in the editing room.

But on stage, you're all out there together. It's like a high wire act—you all depend on each other. It's like the Flying Walendas.

DEBBIE: *(To* JACKIE*)* One of the Flying Waldendas was born in Buffalo.

JACKIE: Get going, Debbie.

*(*DEBBIE *goes.)*

AMANDA: I'll try to be positive about this, Jackie. I'll give him every benefit of the doubt.

JACKIE: Thank you.

AMANDA: So. Fill me in, please. If he's so wonderful, how can he just come in, on the spur of the moment?

JACKIE: I believe he's between jobs.

AMANDA: What jobs?

JACKIE: He just finished the summer at the Great Lakes Shakespeare Festival.

AMANDA: Shakespeare helps. Did he play any big parts?

JACKIE: A title role.

AMANDA: Good for him. What play?

JACKIE: *Othello.*

(Pause)

AMANDA: *Othello.*

JACKIE: He's very popular here in Buffalo. Lots of people would rather see James than Marty Carr.

AMANDA: What do you call this, in the theater? When you mix up the races?

JACKIE: Non-traditional casting.

AMANDA: One thing about television. They don't do that. Black is black and white is white, out there. For better or worse.

JACKIE: The theater's a more imaginative medium. And our audiences expect that.

AMANDA: Well. What can I say? A nineteenth century land-owning Russian lady has just discovered she has a black brother.

(DEBBIE *returns.*)

DEBBIE: He's on his way.

JACKIE: Give him a chance, Amanda.

AMANDA: Of course I'll give him a chance. I happen to think I'm not a prejudiced person. Now let's say no more about it till I've seen him act.

(ROY *returns.*)

ROY: Tania has found several costume possibilities for the picture....

JACKIE: Great.

ROY: And Kenny will come in for the lights. And... (*Another pink slip*) Ginny took this message from Bill Segal.

JACKIE: (*To* AMANDA) The chairman of our board.

ROY: (*Reading with difficulty*) Ginny's penmanship is appalling. The Segals want to take everyone to dinner tonight next door at the City Grill..

JACKIE: (*To* AMANDA) They want to meet our star.

AMANDA: Oh dear.

JACKIE: They're good folks, the Segals. And knowing Bill, he'll also round up some other civilians. Theater-lovers, all. Occasionally heavy-going. But they keep us alive.

AMANDA: We should do it, then.

ROY: I'll tell him we might be quite a crowd.

JACKIE: Knowing Bill, he'll say the more the merrier.

ROY: *(Carefully picking up model)* I'll strike our model before somebody breaks it.. *(Goes)*

JACKIE: Meanwhile, Amanda, you and I need to do a little private business. Want to go to my office?

AMANDA: Could we do it here? I need to get used to my old nursery.

JACKIE: Fine. *(Opening her bag)* Grab a seat somewhere.

DEBBIE: Anyone want coffee or anything?

AMANDA: Is there such a thing in Buffalo as chai? Or is that too L A?

DEBBIE: There's some down in the Green Room. *(She hurries off.)*

JACKIE: *(Settling in)* Now for the tough stuff. Your agent hasn't been very communicative lately.

AMANDA: He doesn't want me to do this.

JACKIE: No kidding.

AMANDA: It's strictly a money thing. He thinks I should do more television.

JACKIE: Do you want to?

AMANDA: It's so tiring, television. You throw yourself into it, you reach out, but nothing comes back. .

JACKIE: You're hungry for an audience.

AMANDA: Starved !

JACKIE: We're developing a good one here....
(Handing her a sheet of paper) Your bio, by the way.
For the program. We tinkered a little with what your agent sent us.

AMANDA: Uh oh. *(Putting on her glasses, reading the bio)*
May I have a pencil, please?

JACKIE: *(Handing her one)* Here.

AMANDA: *(Crossing things out)* No... No...and no.

JACKIE: What's wrong?

AMANDA: No dates, please. I was born and went to
school here. Period.... And no on the private school.
That makes people think I'm a shallow Wasp with a
drinking problem. Which of course I am. *(Reads some
more)* And don't say I "immediately" won a Drama
Desk Award when I went to New York... I spent six
years out and around first..

JACKIE: I'll fix that....

AMANDA: Regionals, summer theaters, showcases.
I worked with the best. Gerorge Grizzard, Frannie
Sternhagen. We did Shakespeare, and—

JACKIE: We say all that.

AMANDA: *(Looking)* So you do. Later on. Put it up front,
please. I did a lot before Hollywood nabbed me...

JACKIE: *(Taking back the bio; making notes)* ...and where
you went on to win your two Academy Award
nominations.

AMANDA: Eventually. For supporting player...

JACKIE: And three Emmys.

AMANDA: Haven't done much of anything lately.

JACKIE: You were on the tube the other night.

AMANDA: Just a re-run. Tiny residuals. Playing that
judge. Everybody does judges when they need money.
Which I do. But you needn't say that..

JACKIE: Of course not.

AMANDA: I'm broke, frankly. *(Indicating her script)*
Like Madame Ranevskaya. I never could save much,
what with the house in Hollywood Hills and the
inevitable shrink. And you probably read somewhere
how one of the men I married walked off with my
savings. Which is almost a cliché out there. And—
(Checking bio) Do you mention my daughter?

JACKIE: Should I?

AMANDA: No. She's in and out of institutions.

JACKIE: I didn't know that.

AMANDA: Manic-depressive. Now they say bi-polar
issues. Sometimes I think she's just plain nuts.

JACKIE: I'm sorry.

AMANDA: Any way you slice it, she's expensive.
Which is another reason why I took this job.

JACKIE: For the money? Get serious.

AMANDA: A play could get me going again. It
happened with Kate Hepburn and Angela Lansbury.
They came back and did plays, and went on to write
their own ticket..

JACKIE: True enough.

AMANDA: So I've been thinking about that. And about
how I need... *(Indicating the stage)* ...this again. *(Reaches
out toward the auditorium)* And them, God love them!
So when you called and said, "Come home. And do a
play *about* coming home," that was it. And it can lead
to bigger things down the line.

JACKIE: For all of us.

AMANDA: And I might be able to do something about
my daughter. And my grandson.

JACKIE: Grandson?

AMANDA: During one of her mood swings,
my daughter managed to deposit on my doorstep
an adorable little boy. Along with a nanny who is
introducing him to the lilting linguistics of rural Peru.

JACKIE: I didn't know you were a grandmother.

AMANDA: I am, and if you mention it anywhere,
I'll throttle you with my bare hands.

JACKIE: O K, O K.

AMANDA: I do not do grandmothers, Jackie. Mothers,
yes. Grandmothers, no way. Which is what I told
my agent. When I said I was considering a play,
he frantically put me up for a stupid sit-com at Fox.
Recurring role, minimum pay—three Emmys
notwithstanding. A character named Granny
Sweetpants. Can you believe it? They even stole
the name from Li'l Abner.

JACKIE: Sounds grim.

AMANDA: I met the writers—a couple of kids fresh out
of kindergarten. They wanted me to wear a gray fright
wig and come into a suburban kitchen, and make jokes
about Viagra. I said Thanks but no thanks, gentlemen.
I am returning to the stage. I'm playing Madame Lubov
Ranevskaya in *The Cherry Orchard* at a distinguished
regional theatah..

JACKIE: You didn't say Buffalo.

AMANDA: People laugh when you say Buffalo.

JACKIE: I want to change that, goddammit.

AMANDA: Anyway, that's why I came back. *(Acts)*
"To my nursery! My own sweet, wonderful room!
I slept here as a child.... And here I am, like a child
again."

*(DEBBIE comes in with the herb tea in a paper take-out cup.
AMANDA takes the tea.)*

AMANDA: "And Varya's just the same, like a nun."...

DEBBIE: That's almost it.

AMANDA: Thank you, Debbie.

JACKIE: Give Tania a hand with Amanda's costume, will you, Debbie.?

DEBBIE: Of course! I love all this multi-tasking. *(She goes.)*

JACKIE: One final thing.

AMANDA: What?

JACKIE: Me. You probably know that with you here, a number of New York producers are coming up to look us over.

AMANDA: My agent mentioned that.

JACKIE: Yes well, that might be another reason why he's holding back on the contract....

AMANDA: I don't get it.

JACKIE: There's a clause about me, which says if the show goes to New York, I go with it.

AMANDA: Why wouldn't you?

JACKIE: Because the theater is an increasingly risky business, and I'm not much of a name.

AMANDA: Oh now...

JACKIE: I don't want some Mike Nichols type taking over, Amanda. I want that New York seal of approval, to give this theater some real clout. One of the bad things about Buffalo is that people here have never really known how to get together. We all huddle in our corners and blame each other for what's gone wrong. Poles, Irish, Italians, Blacks, Jews—and you WASPs are the worst. Now you no longer run things, you've turned your back on the whole mess!

AMANDA: Or run off to Hollywood.

JACKIE: All I know is a first-rate theater here could help pull us together, like the Bills or the Sabres—but at a somewhat higher level.

AMANDA: I'm all for a better Buffalo.

JACKIE: So I wish you'd call this agent of yours, and say I want a signed something which says if this show goes to New York, I go, too.

AMANDA: *(Getting up)* Amen to that.

JACKIE: Oh I have personal reasons, too.

AMANDA: Don't let me pry, but what?

JACKIE: Since I've been home, I've—met someone. She works in the gift shop at the art gallery. We want to be together, but she's scared of losing her kids to the Republican rat she was married to.

AMANDA: How old are the kids?

JACKIE: Teenagers. Both. And retro in spades...

AMANDA: Ouch. The most intolerant group in the world.

JACKIE: Yes, but if I return from New York with a big, fat success under my belt, they might come around. I want to stand up proud with Beth right beside me, and say to those kids, "Hey, look, guys, I'm good at what I do, and I love your mother, and you're lucky as hell to have me involved."

AMANDA: Which they are.

JACKIE: So you're the key to the domestic tranquility of Western New York, Amanda.

AMANDA: Yipes, as Granny Sweetpants would say. I'll call my agent. *(Going)* My cell's in my dressing room.

JACKIE: Reception's better in the green room.

(AMANDA *goes.* JACKIE *begins to fuss with the sightlines of a particular chair.* ROY *comes on with more messages.*)

ROY: James Johnson seemed pissed off on the phone.

JACKIE: Because he knows it's an audition.

ROY: *(Fanning pink slips)* And these were on your desk.

JACKIE: *(As she carefully adjusts the chair)* Shoot.

ROY: *(Reading)* A note from Bruce in the box office says single ticket sales are way up for *The Cherry Orchard*.

JACKIE: Thanks to Amanda... How about overall subscriptions?

ROY: He doesn't say.

JACKIE: He would have said. *(Eyeing chair)* The sightlines are wrong here. *(She again changes its position.)*

ROY: *(A hand-written letter)* Mrs Montesano in Williamsville is worried about the language in Chekhov.

JACKIE: What language?

ROY: She was the one who objected to *Glen Gary Glen Ross*.

JACKIE: I'll write her a polite little note saying this one's clean as a fucking whistle.

ROY: And Fiona Ortez called from New York.

JACKIE: Uh-oh.

ROY: She's just had a baby.

JACKIE: Our innocent little Anya? I thought she was single.

ROY: She is.

JACKIE: She told me she'd lose weight.

ROY: She has.

JACKIE: We'll have to recast.

ROY: She wants to bring it along.

JACKIE: A new baby? Impossible.

ROY: Her mother will come and baby-sit. If we pay her way.

JACKIE: This is blackmail.

ROY: You could use the travel money you save with James Johnson.

JACKIE: The Lenox won't allow children.

ROY: I checked the contract. It says, "actors may keep small pets."

JACKIE: Which means?

ROY: She can smuggle the baby in, in a cat-carrier.

JACKIE: You told her that?

ROY: She's willing to try.

JACKIE: Okey-dokey... What else?

ROY: I also checked your voice mail. A message from Beth, saying she's free for dinner.

JACKIE: I have to eat with the Segals. *(Deciding)* I'll ask her to join us.

ROY: Won't her kids get wind of it?

JACKIE: I hope they do. They'll hear their mother sat next to a T V star.

ROY: That's a start anyway.

JACKIE: That's a big start.

ROY: *(Singing slyly)* Buffalo Gal, won't you come out tonight?

JACKIE: You'll be there, I hope.

ROY: I'm due to eat with my mom.

JACKIE: Bring her along. She's so deep.

ROY: Deep? My mother?

JACKIE: That furrowed brow... That ironic smile...

ROY: She's deaf, remember? When you speak to her, she can't here. So she tries to be aggressively ambiguous. (*He demonstrates.*)

(AMANDA *returns.*)

AMANDA: I got my agent at lunch. He said, if the production stays the same, you will get full directorial credit.

JACKIE: But if some producer wants to change the lighting, I could get fucked.

AMANDA: I told him *The Cherry Orchard* was all your idea.

JACKIE: What did he say to that?

AMANDA: He said *The Cherry Orchard* was all Chekhov's idea.

JACKIE: Funny guy.

ROY: (*Indicating his clipboard*) I'll deal with this stuff. (*He goes quickly.*)

JACKIE: I think this chair should be a little more down right.

AMANDA: My agent also told me something else.

JACKIE: Sit in this chair. Can audience right see you there?

AMANDA: (*Sitting*) That T V show I told you about? They've brought in some new writers. Granny Sweetpants is now Granny Glamour-Puss. She has a young lover and shops at Bergdorf's.

JACKIE: They're obviously interested.

AMANDA: They're always interested when you turn them down. They'd have to triple the money to interest me.

JACKIE: How about the part? Does that interest you?

AMANDA: Not much. I'm sure she still says sappy things. She just looks better saying them.

JACKIE: So where do you stand?

AMANDA: I remember one time I was staying with my grandmother and this rather odd-ball boy asked me to some dance. I mean, he wasn't

terribly popular or anything, but I liked him, so I said sure. And later this other boy, this hot-shot hockey player asked me, too. I wanted to ditch the first boy and go with the hockey player. But my grandmother wouldn't let me. She said I had given my word, and I couldn't break it. So I went with the boy who asked me first. And for that, my grandmother gave me...this. *(She takes off a small gold necklace and shows it to* JACKIE.) I dug it out and wore today specially. To remind me.

JACKIE: *(Reading the pendant)* Buffalo Gal.

AMANDA: For not backing out.

JACKIE: Ah.

AMANDA: I should add that I had a wonderful time with the oddball at the dance.

JACKIE: *(Handing back the necklace)* I hope you'll have a wonderful time with us oddballs in this play, Amanda....

AMANDA: Hey. I like to think I'm an oddball, too.

*(*DEBBIE *comes on.)*

DEBBIE: James Johnson is here.

AMANDA: Oh Lord.

JACKIE: Tell him to come on out.

(DEBBIE *goes off.*)

AMANDA: *(Low to* JACKIE*)* Now I suddenly feel very condescending. Like Queen Elizabeth receiving a delegate from Nigeria or some place.

JACKIE: You asked for it.

AMANDA: I know. No wonder we have agents. So we're not put so totally on the spot.

(DEBBIE *comes in with* JAMES, *a good-looking African American, about* AMANDA's *age.*)

DEBBIE: Mister James Johnson.

AMANDA: *(Extending her hand, too grandly)* How do you do.

(They shake hands).

JAMES: *(Immediately quoting Chekhov)* "The train was two hours late. What do you think of that? What a way to manage things?"

AMANDA: Train? There are still trains running here?

DEBBIE: That's his first line in the play.

AMANDA: Oh the *play*! ...Of course. Very good, very good! I believed you immediately.

JAMES: *(Looking at a piece of prop furniture; again quoting Chekhov)* "Do you know, Lubov, how old this bookcase is? Last week I pulled out the bottom drawer, and there was the date, burned into it! It was made exactly a hundred years ago. Think of that. We could celebrate its centenary. True, it's an inanimate object, but nevertheless, a bookcase..."

AMANDA: *(To* DEBBIE*)* Quickly. What do I say?

DEBBIE: *(Finding her place in the script)* You don't say anything.

AMANDA: Thank God.

DEBBIE: *(Reads, to* JAMES*)* Pischik says, "A hundred
years! Just imagine!"

JAMES: "Yes! That's something! ...Dear honored
bookcase, hail to you who for more than a century
have served the glorious ideals of goodness and justice!
Your silent summons to fruitful toil has never
weakened in all these hundred years..." *(To* JACKIE*)*
Chekhov asks for tears here.... You want tears?

JACKIE: Sure. Give us tears.

JAMES: *(Resumes speech, through tears)* "...sustaining,
through successive generations of our family, courage
and faith in a better future, and fostering in us ideals of
goodness and social consciousness..." *(Wipes his eyes)*

DEBBIE: *(To* AMANDA*)* Here's where you come in....

AMANDA: Hold it. *(To* JAMES*)* You seem vaguely
familiar. Have we worked together?

JAMES: We have.

AMANDA: Back in the eighties? That Hallmark Special?
For Martin Luther King Day?

JAMES: Nope.

AMANDA: Give me a hint. Where did we meet?

JAMES: Here.

AMANDA: In Buffalo? When?

JAMES: A while back.

AMANDA: *(Looking at him)* Don't tell me...

JAMES: I won't.

AMANDA: *(Suddenly)* Of course! At Miss Keeler's !
You were the... Now wait...I know who you are....
You're Jimmy Johnson!

JAMES: The same.

DEBBIE: Who was Miss Keeler?

AMANDA: She ran this acting class over on Lafayette Avenue.

JAMES: Saturday mornings. For kids.

AMANDA: Kids who could get *in*. We had to audition....

JAMES: *(Wryly)* Just like here.

JACKIE: We call this a meeting, James.

AMANDA: No it isn't! It's more than that!

DEBBIE: Aristotle would call it a recognition scene! A change from ignorance to knowledge.

JACKIE: Quiet, Debby...

AMANDA: Miss Keeler's classes were quite a thing. They got me started.

JAMES: Me, too.

AMANDA: My mother sent me to get the theater "out of my system."

JAMES: Mine got me a scholarship there. She caught me playing Superman in front of the T V wearing her best bedspread, and thought I had talent....

AMANDA: Which you did.

JAMES: It was the first time I'd been west of Main Street.

AMANDA: I've never been east of it. *(To others)* We'd put on plays. We did *Tom Sawyer* together!

JAMES: You played Becky Thatcher.

AMANDA: And you did Injun Joe.

JAMES: "I'm gonna catch-um that nosey Tom Sawyer and put a knife in his meddlin' heart!"

AMANDA: *(To others)* See? He was marvelous.

JAMES: You weren't bad yourself.

AMANDA: Thank you.

(ROY *enters.*)

ROY: Jim-Jim!

JAMES: Roy-Boy!

(*They embrace.*)

AMANDA: This is exciting! (*To* JAMES) Why didn't you say you knew me?

JAMES: I didn't think you'd remember.

AMANDA: I remember one time you did this big leap off this rock! (*To others*) He was always taking these risks.

JAMES: I was playing a frog. When I turned into the prince, a white boy took over.

AMANDA: No! Did that happen?

JAMES: It did.

AMANDA: Oh Miss Keeler.

JAMES: She was O K, though. Miss Keeler.

AMANDA: She taught us to breathe.

JAMES: And to... (*Imitating*) "enunciate."

AMANDA: (*Laughing*) Yes. To "enunciate." And to project.

JAMES: (*Imitating*) "Project, children! So they can hear you all the way to the back row!" And...

AMANDA & JAMES: (*Simultaneously*) "Take the stage!" (*And they take it.*)

AMANDA: "Take the stage, children! Remember to take the stage." Oh Jimmy, were you there when Katharine Cornell visited the class and showed us how to cross? Remember? She said to take aim for a chair or

something, and then slide sideways, like this.
(She demonstrates a big, melodramatic way of crossing.)
Of course she was at the end of her career by then.
And had a bad leg. *(She hoists her leg into place.)*

JACKIE: Nobody acts that way anymore. It's like
Chekhov, talking about the jam they used to make
from the cherry orchard. Someone says, "they knew
the way to do it then." And someone else says."
Why don't they do it that way now?"

JAMES: "They've forgotten. No one remembers."

JACKIE: That's the line.

AMANDA: You remember Katharine Cornell, don't you,
Jimmy?

JAMES: I wasn't there then. Miss Keeler let me go. She
said I was getting too old.

AMANDA: Too old for what?

JAMES: Being with girls.

AMANDA: Oh. *(To JACKIE)* That was when the fig-leaf
was still on the statue of David.

JAMES: You stayed on, huh.

AMANDA: For a few years. Until I could play with the
grown-ups.

DEBBIE: This is all very interesting. *(To JACKIE)* May I
say something here?

JACKIE: If you have to, Debbie.

DEBBIE: I just want to say that these amateur theater
groups were once a mainspring of American drama.
They gave audiences a taste for plays and the habit
of going to them.

JACKIE: *(Dryly)* My, my.

AMANDA: That's fascinating, Debbie.

DEBBIE: I'm writing my senior thesis on it. I'm arguing for more government support at the local level.

AMANDA: I agree wholeheartedly.

ROY: I'll check on that costume. *(He exits.)*

JAMES: *(To* AMANDA*)* I saw you again, you know. Later on.

AMANDA: Here in Buffalo?

JAMES: When your grandmother was sick.

AMANDA: I came back when she was dying.

JAMES: My mama helped take care of her. She was a home health aide..

AMANDA: I remember a Mrs... *(Looks at him)* ...Johnson!

JAMES: That was my mama.

AMANDA: Why didn't she say she was your mother?

JAMES: I told her not to.

AMANDA: But why?

JAMES: I wasn't ready for a recognition scene at that time.

JACKIE: James...

JAMES: She should know. *(To* AMANDA*)* I was just out of jail at that time.

AMANDA: Oh dear.

JAMES: They caught me coming back from Toronto with a bag in my pocket.

JACKIE: Talk about racial profiling.

JAMES: In this case, they were right. Going through customs, I was high a kite. , I had just been canned in Toronto for turning the butler in *The Little Foxes* into a total hophead

AMANDA: Oh God. Tell me about it.

JAMES: You too?

AMANDA: Vodka. Ever hear about that guest spot when I played Mary Tyler Moore's alcoholic sister?

JAMES: You played it sauced?

AMANDA: I went for realism. They decided not to make it a recurring role.

JAMES: How'd you kick your habit?

AMANDA: Good old WASP will-power. How about you?

JAMES: You won't believe this.

AMANDA: Try me.

JAMES: One night, when I came round to pick up my mama at your grandmother's, I was waiting in the car when you came to the door.

AMANDA: I was a mess, with my grandmother dying upstairs.

JAMES: All I saw was one successful lady, standing in the light. I told my probation officer I was ready to get serious, and he got me into rehab. And I'm telling you, Amanda, I've been clean ever since. And working mostly when I want to. Of course, by then the regional theaters were going big time. And into... *(Indicating at* JACKIE*)* Non-traditional casting. Which means I could do O'Neill and Ibsen and Shakespeare.

JACKIE: *(To* AMANDA*)* Last year he did Marco for me, in *A View from the Bridge*...

JAMES: I blew them away.

JACKIE: You did! The way you picked up that chair!

JAMES: *(Demonstrating with a chair)* See? I do furniture. I don't do frogs any more.

AMANDA: Why do you stay in Buffalo, James?

JAMES: Because my mama's here. And my lady's here. And there's a theater here.

AMANDA: The theater gives you a base, doesn't it? It anchors you.

JAMES: Hell, baby, it's saved my life. *(Going to the "window")* "The cherry orchard is all white."

AMANDA: Oh, the play.

JAMES: "Have you forgotten it, Lubov? That's the long alley that runs straight, straight as an arrow."

AMANDA: Oh yes!

JAMES: "How it shines on moonlit nights, do you remember? Don't tell me you've forgotten."

(The lighting changes to highlight the scene)

JACKIE: *(Softly, indicating the lights)* Kenny's here.

AMANDA: *(Going to the "window")* I know this part, I know this. " Oh My childhood, my innocent childhood. I used to sleep in this nursery—I used to look out into the orchard... All, all white!"

(AMANDA her head on JAMES's shoulder as they look out.)

AMANDA: Oh my orchard! After the dark, rainy autumn and cold winter, you are young again, and full of happiness ..."

JAMES: "Yes, and the orchard will be sold to pay our debts, strange as it may seem ..."

AMANDA: "Look! There is our poor mother walking in the orchard...all in white... There she is!"

JAMES: "Where?"

AMANDA: "There's no one there, I just imagined it. To the right, where the path turns toward the arbor, there's a little white tree, leaning over, that looks like a woman..."

JAMES: Looks like Miss Keeler, leaning over a script.

AMANDA: It is! It's Miss Keeler! After all these years!

(AMANDA *and* JAMES *laugh.*)

AMANDA: Jimmy Johnson, will you be in *The Cherry Orchard* with me?

JAMES: Sure.

AMANDA: *(Suddenly embracing him)* My dear, dear brother.

JAMES: My long lost sister!

DEBBIE: *(Flipping through the script)* Where are we? I can't find those lines.

JAMES: They're not in the script. *(He starts out.)*

JACKIE: Come back around six, James. The Segals are buying dinner over at the City Grill.

JAMES: Can I bring my lady?

JACKIE: Why not?

JAMES: She speaks mostly Spanish, remember.

JACKIE: Bienvenida.

JAMES: I'll talk to her. *(He goes.)*

AMANDA: *(Looking after him)* He's the best!

JACKIE: I told you.

DEBBIE: Am I invited to the Segal's party?

JACKIE: The more the merrier.

DEBBIE: Can I bring my thesis advisor?

JACKIE: *(Immediately)* No.

DEBBIE: Didn't think so.

AMANDA: Oh more and more, it's feeling so delicious to come home!

(ROY *comes in, carrying a manila envelope.*)

ROY: *(To* JACKIE*)* Tania's almost ready with the costume.

JACKIE: And Kenny's here. *(Calls up)* Thanks, Kenny.

AMANDA: *(Calling up)* Plenty of pink, please, Kenny. If you've got a special, hit me on the left....

ROY: *(To* AMANDA*)* By the way, we got a call from your agent. He couldn't get you on your cell. *(Hands her a pink slip)*

AMANDA: That's because I turned it off.

JACKIE: Amen to that.

ROY: Let me. I majored in hieroglyphics *(Reading it for her)* "Further development from Fox."

JACKIE: Here we go again.

AMANDA: Hollywood talk. *(Tears up note; hands pieces to* ROY*)* If he calls again, I am deep in rehearsal.

ROY: Gotcha. *(Handing* AMANDA *the manila envelope)* And this was delivered to Frank at the stage door.

AMANDA: For me?

JACKIE: A present from a fan?

AMANDA: It's a... *(Shows it)* ...C D.

JACKIE: Read the label.

ROY: Let me. *(Taking it, reading)* "For Amanda, from Danny."

AMANDA: Danny Rubin.

JACKIE: Danny the dentist?

AMANDA: Maybe it's a lecture on root canals.

JACKIE: Want to listen to it? While we're waiting on your costume?

AMANDA: I'm almost tempted.

JACKIE: *(To* ROY*)* Does Sandy ever come in on Mondays?

ROY: I think he's here. Working on ourdoor sounds for Chekhov. *(Calls off)* Are you here, Sandy?

(We hear barking dogs over the sound system.)

JACKIE: *(To* AMANDA*)* Sandy's here. Want him to play this?

AMANDA: Oh I don't know *(Looking at C D)* Actually I think I know what this is.

DEBBIE: What?

AMANDA: A love song he wrote.

DEBBIE: I love love songs.

AMANDA: You want to hear some adolescent caterwauling?

JACKIE: Why not?

AMANDA: Oh hell. I'm too tempted to say no.

*(*AMANDA *hands it to* ROY*)*

ROY: *(Taking it; calling off)* A job for you, Sandy. *(Goes off)*

AMANDA: *(To* JACKIE*)* Danny and I knew each other as teen-agers. He went to the Nichols School—that's a private school for boys. And I went to what was once called the Buffalo Female Academy. But he had written this musical ...

*(*ROY *comes back on.)*

ROY: Ready to go.

AMANDA: Prepare yourselves for some teen-age trivia...

(Over the sound system, we hear a rather lush piano introduction.)

JACKIE: That's his music?

AMANDA: His uncle hired a professional pianist and rented a studio...

(A BOY'S VOICE is heard)

BOY'S VOICE: Say When...
We'll meet again...

AMANDA: That's Danny... When he was young.

BOY'S VOICE: Say where...
And I'll be there...

Say why...
We said goodbye,
I wish I knew...

AMANDA: Now comes guess who...

(A sweet young girl's voice)

GIRL'S VOICE: Say how...
You're doing now,

Say who...
You're talking to...

Say what...
To bring you back
I have to do...

AMANDA: I love what he does with the bridge....

BOY'S VOICE: I'm lost when I'm alone,
I'm hopeless on my own...
I'd like to close my eyes and count to ten...
And then...

BOY'S & GIRL'S VOICES: I'd open them to see
You coming back to me ...

(AMANDA *is lost in her memories as the* BOY *and* GIRL *sing on.*)

BOY'S & GIRL'S VOICES:
Ah when, oh when, say when."

(The song ends. A pause)

ROY: It should be "Say who*m* you're talking to."

AMANDA: It didn't rhyme.

DEBBIE: I loved it.

AMANDA: Excuse me, but would you mind if I took a short break? Because I really think I'm going to cry. *(She hurries out.)*

JACKIE: *(Looking after her; dryly)* Shit! Just what we need to help her concentrate. Some long lost dentist.

ROY: *(Going to the coffee stand)* Anyone want coffee?

JACKIE: I do.

DEBBIE: No thanks.

JACKIE: Good song, anyway.

ROY: Very retro. *(He goes off.)*

DEBBIE: I loved it. *(Pause)* Should I go see if I can—?

JACKIE: No.

DEBBIE: Things seem so quiet, suddenly.

JACKIE: This is like one of those filler scenes in plays from the Thirties where everyone stands around waiting for the star to come back on stage.

DEBBIE: That's very interesting because you know what?

JACKIE: *(Patiently)* What, Debbie?

DEBBIE: All theater has to do with invoking some god. Greek theater began as a prayer to the god Dionysus. Today our gods are Hollywood celebrities. And so what we're really doing right now is trying to invoke our own local god, Amanda, hoping she'll reappear in our sacred space..

JACKIE: When do you graduate?

(ROY *returns.*)

ROY: While we're invoking Dionysus, Debbie, do you suppose you could straighten up the sacred space?

DEBBIE: O K. (*She cleans up.*)

JACKIE: And Roy, maybe you could set up the rehearsal schedule, now we know we've got James. Does he have any other commitments?

ROY: (*Checking his laptop*) He records for the blind, two mornings a week.

JACKIE: Find out when.

ROY: I already have. There's no problem.

JACKIE: (*Taking her script out her bag*) Meanwhile Jackie here better study her script.

DEBBIE: Do you feel better about Amanda, Jackie?

JACKIE: I'll feel better the Sunday after Thanksgiving when she gives her final performance.

ROY: (*Looking off*) Ssshh. She's coming back!

(AMANDA *comes on, drying her eyes.*)

AMANDA: Sorry.

JACKIE: Everything all right?

AMANDA: That was just a slight attack of nostalgia. Which sounds like a disease, doesn't it, Debbie? Take two aspirin. For headaches, neuritis, and nostalgia.

JACKIE: We all have our soft spots.

AMANDA: Here's the thing. He had written this musical, and got my name from Miss Keeler, and called me up out of the blue and

asked me to be in it. It was the first joint project between our single-sex schools.

DEBBIE: See how theater neutralizes gender issues....

AMANDA: We put it on in the boy's gymnasium. Dan directed it himself. It had this dumb book, but some of the songs were quite good. Everyone thought this one was the best.

JACKIE: I liked it.

DEBBIE: We all liked it.

AMANDA: And of course by then Danny and I had fallen madly in love, as people do in show business.

JACKIE: Been there...

ROY: Done that.

AMANDA: We couldn't see enough of each other. Until my mother broke it up.

DEBBIE: Because he was Jewish?

AMANDA: Because she caught us in bed together.

DEBBIE: Oooh!

AMANDA: I'm sure the Jewish thing was part of it, too. My father said he was pushy. Which he was. And which I loved about him. He thought we should both quit school and go into the theater together. My parents said it was an unstable and vulgar occupation.

JACKIE: No shit.

AMANDA: Of course, the sex thing was the last straw. We used to meet in the chauffeur's room in the barn behind my grandmother's house. Remember? I showed you, Jackie.

JACKIE: The scene of the crime.

AMANDA: By that time, the chauffeur was long gone,
but the cot was still there, and we went there all
summer. Finally some neighbor saw us going in,
and told my mother, and she walked in on us. Right
in the middle of things.

DEBBIE: What did she say?

JACKIE: She said "Don't get up".

AMANDA: (Laughing) Not quite. She got right on the
telephone, and found this crummy boarding school
to ship me off to.

JACKIE: What about him?

AMANDA: Dan? Oh his parents were just as bad. They
were pushing him towards college and dental school
and nice Jewish girls. I was an immoral shiksa who had
led him astray. We tried to keep things going in the fall.
Or at least he did. Letters and phone calls and stuff.
But things kind of petered out.

JACKIE: As things do, in the theater.

AMANDA: I hated boarding school, and quit college
after the first semester, and finally said the hell with
my parents, and took acting classes in New York—
which my grandmother paid for, by the way. And you
know what? She told me, before she died, that the
whole experience had been good for me.

JACKIE: Why did she say that?

AMANDA: Because it taught me to follow my feelings.
And with that thought, I have to make another
dramatic exit, because Tania wants to sew me into
that costume. (She goes.)

ROY: I'll get my camera,... (He goes)

JACKIE: *(Following him)* I'll be in my office. Let me know when you're all set up.

(They both go off.)

(DEBBIE remains on stage, fussing with the script.)

(DAN comes in, hesitantly, from somewhere. He is a nice looking man, about AMANDA's age.)

DAN: That was my song.

DEBBIE: *(Startled)* Excuse me.

DAN: I was waiting by the stage door, and I heard my song.

DEBBIE: Are you Doctor Rubin?

DAN: Robbins.

DEBBIE: You shouldn't be here, sir.

DAN: You might tell the guard at the door I have every right to hear my own song. I had to sneak in through the fire-escape.

DEBBIE: *(Starting out)* I'll get the stage manager.

DAN: Just tell me one thing. Did she listen to it?

DEBBIE: We all listened to it.

DAN: Did she like it?

DEBBIE: It made her cry.

DAN: Knew it! Could I see her?

DEBBIE: We're kind of busy here.

DAN: Just to say hello.

DEBBIE: I'll check.

DAN: I'll wait here.

DEBBIE: Please don't touch anything.

DAN: Me? I'd never do that. I'm a theater man, too, you know. I used to be very involved in the theater.

DEBBIE: I know. *(Starts out, comes back)* Actually I'm writing my thesis on the importance of amateur theater in America.

DAN: That's interesting.

DEBBIE: I'm arguing that Buffalo audiences must have enjoyed seeing people like you or Amanda perform on the local stage, just as Athenian audiences cheered their relatives dancing in the choruses of Sophocles.

DAN: Oh yes?

DEBBIE: And community theaters were once an important source of talent for Broadway.

DAN: Uh, would you—?

DEBBIE: Katharine Cornell, Henry Fonda, even Marlon Brando, all began in this way.

DAN: Would you see—?

DEBBIE: So over the years, this grassroots theater brought a kind of homegrown authenticity to Broadway, which was also absorbing the vulgar vitality of vaudeville and burlesque.

DAN: Would you see about Amanda, please?

DEBBIE: Oh. Yes. Right. *(She goes off.)*

*(*DEBBIE *hurries off.* DAN *paces nervously, does a few, furtive dance steps. Then* JACKIE *comes on,* DEBBIE *following behind.)*

JACKIE: Doctor Rubin?

DAN: *(Regaining his composure)* Robbins.

JACKIE: Jaqueline Sinofsky.

*(*DAN *and* JACKIE *shake hands.)*

DAN: You're doing great things for Buffalo.

JACKIE: I try.

DAN: We come to a lot of your shows, my wife and I. We saw *Doubt* and *Proof* and *The Vagina Monologues*....

JACKIE: Thank you, but I'm afraid you'll have to leave.

DAN: I hear my song made her cry.

JACKIE: She's a little stressed out. Returning to the stage and all.

DAN: Still it got to her, didn't it? It got to her.

(ROY comes on with his camera and tripod. He also carries an old "For Sale" sign on a stanchion)

ROY *(Indicating the sign)* Look what I found in the prop room.

JACKIE: You see, Doctor Robbins? We need to use the stage now.

DAN: Could I see her?

JACKIE: Not the best time.

DAN: Just for five minutes.

JACKIE: We're setting up for a photo shoot.

DAN: I can't just walk away from this.

ROY: We're kind of pressed for time, sir.

DAN: Couldn't I watch, at least?

JACKIE: You might distract her. *(Calls up to the lighting booth)* Show us what you've got, Kenny!

(The area for the photo is bathed in a warm glow. ROY and DEBBIE finish setting up a space for the photograph.)

JACKIE: Looks good.

DAN: Looks great!

JACKIE: Doctor, please. How would you like it if I stood around, watching you fill a tooth.

(DAN *shrugs*)

ROY: Sir: the director is asking you to leave!

DAN: All right, all right. I just wanted to— (*He looks off.*) Oh hey!

(AMANDA *comes on into the theatrical light. She wears a lovely nineteenth century gown, and looks terrific.*)

DAN: Amanda.

JACKIE: The guy won't leave.

DAN: I can't.

AMANDA: (*Shielding her eyes in the bright light*) Dan?

DAN: The same.

AMANDA: You look different, Dan.

DAN: You look sensational.

AMANDA: This is just a costume.

JACKIE: Let's take the picture and then talk, O K?

AMANDA: Could you give us a minute, Jackie? Please?

JACKIE: Fine. I only work here. (*To others*) Exeunt omnes, gang.

(*Low to* DEBBIE *as they go out*)

JACKIE: This is going to be a big problem.

(ROY *crosses angrily in front of* DAN *and goes. Pause*)

AMANDA: Well, well. So you're a full-fledged dentist.

DAN: I've got an office out in Eggertsville.

AMANDA: That's where people live now, isn't it? I mean, more of them.

DAN: It's a decent suburb.

AMANDA: Decent, is it? Your parents must be pleased.

DAN: They're dead.

AMANDA: Oh I'm sorry. So are mine.

DAN: I remember reading your grandmother's obituary.

AMANDA: That was a long time ago.

DAN: I know you were fond of her.

AMANDA: I loved her.

DAN: I know that. I respect that. Goddammit, you look good, Amanda! I mean, you always looked good, and I've seen you in the movies and on T V, but you look even better in real life.

AMANDA: It's the lighting. *(Touching her face)* I'm thinking of getting a little nip and tuck here and there.

DAN: Don't you dare... They said you listened to the song.

AMANDA: I'm amazed you kept it.

DAN: Of course I kept it. And I played it till the tape broke. I repaired it myself, twice, before I finally had it put on C D....

AMANDA: You listen to it a lot?

DAN: Too much maybe. I even sing along with it a little.

AMANDA: I did that just now.

DAN: Want to do it again?

AMANDA: Now?

DAN: Why not? Ask them to play it.

AMANDA: Don't be silly.

DAN: All right, all right.

AMANDA: Did you write any other songs?

DAN: I tried at least. But after you, I went in a different direction.

AMANDA: You sure did. How do you like my teeth?

DAN: *(Taking off his glasses; inspecting her teeth carefully)* Gorgeous.

AMANDA: They better be. They cost thousands.

DAN: Are you married ?

AMANDA: Not now. Was. Three times.

DAN: I know that. I read the magazines in my waiting room. Your husbands were shits, weren't they?

AMANDA: Two were, one was a good man.

DAN: What happened to the good man?

AMANDA: He fell in love with another good man.

DAN: Bummer... So you're free now?

AMANDA: So to speak. I have—large financial obligations.

DAN: So do I. I married an expensive woman. Naomi Satler from Buffalo.

AMANDA: Should I know her?

DAN: Satler's Department Store? *(Singing from the jingle)* 998 Broadway!

AMANDA: Oh right. Is it still there?

DAN: Nothing's still there. *(Pause)* Except Naomi's still there. She went to Radcliffe.

AMANDA: She sounds smart.

DAN: She has her M S W.

AMANDA: Which means?

DAN: Master's Degree in Social Work. And we have three kids. And two grand-kids.

(DAN *takes out his wallet, shows* AMANDA *a picture.*)

AMANDA: Grandchildren! Good grief! At your age! *(Pause)* Well, all right. I have one, too.

DAN: Grandchild? You?

AMANDA: Off the record, please.

DAN: I get it. Because of your career.

AMANDA: What career?

DAN: You've had a fantastic career, Amanda.

AMANDA: Once upon a time.

DAN: All those movies. Those T V shows...

AMANDA: My phone doesn't ring much these days.

DAN: You'll bounce back.

AMANDA: Doing this play might help.

DAN: He's a great writer, Chekhov.

AMANDA: If I can remember his lines.

DAN: They say it comes back, like riding a bicycle.

AMANDA: I wasn't much good at that either.

DAN: You were good at everything.

AMANDA: *(Curtseying)* Thank you, Dan. *(Pause)* There's this sit-com they want me to do.

DAN: Do you like sit-coms?

AMANDA: I like the good ones.

DAN: Is this one good?

AMANDA: No.

DAN: Then don't do it. Hold the fort.

AMANDA: I will. I plan to.

DAN: How come you didn't write me? After you left.

AMANDA: I wrote.

DAN: Not much. Not as much as I did. And when I called, you hardly ever called back.

AMANDA: I got involved.

DAN: With what? Some other guy?

AMANDA: That was later.

DAN: So how come you blew me off? You didn't even come home from boarding school that first Thanksgiving.

AMANDA: What a memory.

DAN: I remember that.

AMANDA: So do I, actually. I had other plans.

DAN: What other plans?

AMANDA: Does it make any difference? After all these years?

DAN: It does to me.

AMANDA: All right. *(Pause)* I didn't come home Thanksgiving vacation because I had an abortion Thanksgiving vacation.

DAN: No.

AMANDA: Yes, Dan.

DAN: Your parents put the pressure on you, right? Your mother found some snazzy Park Avenue doctor to help you out?

AMANDA: My mother never even knew about it. It was my idea, all the way. I wanted to go into the theater and thought a baby would hold me back.

DAN: It would have.

AMANDA: I told everyone I was visiting some friend in Puerto Rico, and off I went, by myself.

DAN: I would have gone with you.

AMANDA: I didn't want that.

DAN: Wow, Amanda. You grew up fast.

AMANDA: I'll tell you this, Dan. I'm big on Pro-Choice, and I chose, all right, but this was no fun. I felt guilty and corrupt. I didn't even want to look at a man for a while.

DAN: Not even me?

AMANDA: Especially not you.

DAN: I'm very sorry about all that. No, really. I am.

AMANDA: So am I. Still. After all these years. When I got married, and finally did have a child, and it turned out she had these problems, I kept thinking she was a punishment for having gotten rid of my first.

DAN: That's horseshit.

AMANDA: That's what my psychiatrist said. But I felt it. And still do.

DAN: Do you still think about me? Ever?

AMANDA: Sometimes.

DAN: Even out in Hollywood?

AMANDA: Whenever I want a part, or a project, I push to make it happen. The way you did, with our show, years ago, back here.

DAN: Me, I had no follow-through. I went into dentistry.

AMANDA: You just followed through in another direction.

DAN: Maybe.

AMANDA: I imagine you're a wonderful dentist.

DAN: I am, actually. I never did an in-lay I didn't like.

(JACKIE *sticks her head in.*)

JACKIE: I hate to interrupt but—

DAN: Five more minutes? For old time's sake?

JACKIE: (*Frustratedly*) Five. And counting. (*She goes off.*)

DAN: Would you have dinner with me tonight

AMANDA: I'm tied up .Some people on the board are taking us out.

DAN: Could I tag along?

AMANDA: I don't think so.

DAN: Professional obligations, right.

AMANDA: Right.

DAN: I want to see more of you.

AMANDA: I see you're still pushy.

DAN: I should have been pushier. When can I see you?

AMANDA: Hey, you're a married man.

DAN: She's thinking of leaving me.... Want to know why?

AMANDA: I doubt if it's any of my business.

DAN: It's because of you.

AMANDA: Oh come on.

DAN: She says she can't compete with you.

AMANDA: I don't remember taking her on.

DAN: She says I've never gotten over you. She claims all I do is boast about our relationship. Which is true, Amanda! I'm a nut case about you! Every movie you were ever in, we went out to see. Every time you're on T V, we stay home to watch.

AMANDA: Why thank you.

DAN: And... *(Pause)* You won't like this...

AMANDA: Try me.

DAN: I go around telling people I slept with you. I do it all the time. People I don't know very well. Last week I told the guy who fixed the furnace. I imagine you think that's a shitty thing to do.

AMANDA: I'll get over it.

DAN: Naomi says she can't compete with a movie star.

AMANDA: Tell her I'm fading fast.

DAN: She said the song was the last straw.

AMANDA: The song?

DAN: When I heard you were coming to Buffalo, I got out the tape and played it over and over again. At one point she tried to throw it into the trash-masher.

AMANDA: Oh dear.

DAN: She says she knows now that I never really loved her, I always loved you, and that's why I changed our name from Rubin to Robbins. To make myself more acceptable to you. Subconsciously.

AMANDA: Now that's just plain silly.

DAN: Her specialty is psychology.

AMANDA: I like the name Rubin better anyway. Maybe because I knew you that way.

DAN: Then I'll change it back.

AMANDA: Slow down, Dan.

DAN: I don't want to slow down. I want to go faster. Listen, Amanda: you're single now, and I could be soon, and you're going to be stuck in Buffalo for—how long?

AMANDA: Seven weeks.

DAN: Seven long weeks! And what are you going to do after rehearsal every night?

AMANDA: Try to learn my lines!

DAN: O K then, after the show opens? What will you do, after you've been to Niagara Falls, and seen the Art Gallery, and checked out a few old friends? You can be with me, that's what.

AMANDA: And cause a divorce. Now please go, Dan.

DAN: Oh look, Amanda. I know we can't turn back the clock. But we could wind up a new one. The kids are out of the nest, and Naomi wants her own space, so let's gather rosebuds, kid. And in seven weeks, if it doesn't work out, we can shake hands, and say goodbye, and that's that. What do you say? Let me walk out of here with some hope.

AMANDA: Why is everyone putting me on the spot today? I've never felt so much pressure in my life! Please!

DAN: O K. I'll go quietly. *(Starts out, stops)* Except...

AMANDA: What?

DAN: Sing the song with me first.

AMANDA: I will not.

DAN: Come on. Do it, then I'm out of here. Forever if you want. I swear.

AMANDA: I'm sorry. No.

(JACKIE comes back out.)

JACKIE: Do it, Amanda. or he'll be here all night. *(She gives a signal toward offstage.)* Hit it, Sandy.

(The piano intro from the tape starts up.)

JACKIE: There's you cue, Doctor. Your big finish.

DAN: *(To* AMANDA, *over the music)* Remember the words?

AMANDA: Not a one.

(Music starts. They might sing along with the BOY'S *and* BOY'S *and* GIRL'S VOICES.*)*

BOY'S VOICE: Say when we'll meet again?...
Say where and I'll be there
Say why we said goodbye, I wish I knew.

GIRL'S VOICE: Say how you're doing now...
Say who you're talking to...
Say what to bring you back I have to do...

(The BOY'S *and* BOY'S *and* GIRL'S VOICES *sing the bridge under the following dialogue:)*

DAN: Here's where we did the dance, remember?

AMANDA: No.

*(*DAN *and* AMANDA *dance conventionally.)*

DAN: Have you seen your grandmother's house?

AMANDA: Yes.

DAN: I drive by now and then.

AMANDA: It's for sale.

DAN: Again?

AMANDA: I wish I could buy it.

DAN: I'd help you. *(He tries a more elaborate step.)* We could live there.

AMANDA: Oh Lord.

*(*DAN *puts his hands on* AMANDAs *waist.)*

AMANDA: Hey! What are you doing?

DAN: Here's where I lift you up....

AMANDA: Don't you dare!

DAN: Actually I've got a bad back.

AMANDA: And I've got a new hip.

DAN: So we won't do that part.

AMANDA: (*Walking away from him*) We won't do any part.

(JACKIE *comes out, giving the cut sign to off and up.*)

JACKIE: Cut it, Sandy!

(*The music stops.* ROY *comes out with his camera, followed by* DEBBIE)

DEBBIE: That was so cool.

JACKIE: Yes it was. Now goodbye, Doctor.

DEBBIE: You two should do a musical. Of "The Cherry Orchard."

JACKIE: (*Dryly*) You could call it "Cherry".

AMANDA: (*rubbing her hip*) It can hurt to go back.

DAN: Yes well, I'm ready to move forward. I'm thinking of giving up dentistry. I'm tired of looking in people's mouths. I'd rather sing.

JACKIE: So people can look in yours?

DAN: O K, O K, but I think all of us should change our lives at least once before we die.

DEBBIE: I'm going to change *my* life. I was planning to go on to the Yale School of Drama, but I think I'm becoming too abstract. I'm going into the working theater instead. The way you did, Amanda.

AMANDA: Can we take this picture, before I go insane. (*She takes her position*)

JACKIE: (*To* DAN) Time to go, Doctor.

DAN: I agree. Amanda, I'm going home right now to talk to Naomi. I plan to follow through this time.

JACKIE: Please show Doctor Robbins the stage door, Debbie.

DEBBIE: O K.

(DAN *and* DEBBIE *go.)*

AMANDA: Oh Lord. He's going to get a messy divorce.

JACKIE: On with the show, gang...

AMANDA: Where do you want me to stand?

JACKIE: Except, before we begin, I should tell you something. Your agent called again.

AMANDA: I told you I don't want to talk to him.

JACKIE: He asked for me.

AMANDA: Oh. *(Pause)* And?

JACKIE: He spelled out your deal.

AMANDA: I don't want to hear.

JACKIE: You're sure?

AMANDA: Positive.

JACKIE: Then I've done my job...

(DEBBIE *has come back on by now. She helps* ROY *with his photo equipment.* JACKIE *checks her script.)*

JACKIE: Now: let's take the moment when you hear the cherry orchard is sold. Chekhov calls for a table and a chair nearby, so that when you hear the news you have something to lean on.

ROY: Debbie...

(DEBBIE *places a table and chair nearby.)*

AMANDA: I suppose he mentioned money.

JACKIE: Not specifically... Move the table a little down right, Debbie, next to the chair.... That looks good.

AMANDA: What then?

(DEBBIE *places it near the chair.*)

JACKIE: Now the "For Sale" sign... (*To* AMANDA*)*
He just said they had met his demands..

AMANDA: Oh yes? Well, there's always some hitch.
Always (*Notices the sign beside her*) Does that sign have
to be right there? It's the house that's for sale, not me.

JACKIE: Move it back, Debbie.

(DEBBIE *does;* ROY *begins to focus his camera.*)

AMANDA: I imagine he wants me to meet with the suits.

JACKIE: He said something about that.

DEBBIE: Who are the suits?

AMANDA: The "suits", Debbie, are the network
executives. They wear suits, and like to meet with
what they call "the talent". I'm "the talent".

JACKIE: (*Calling up to the lighting booth*) Can you hit
that area a little better, Kenny?

(*The lights change on it.*)

JACKIE: Ready, Amanda? Ready, Roy?

AMANDA: (*Striking a pose*) How about this?

JACKIE: (*To* AMANDA*)* It's a little O T T.

AMANDA: I agree.

DEBBIE: What does that mean?

JACKIE: Over. The. Top. (*To* AMANDA*)* You might tone
it down a little.

AMANDA: (*Takes a less dramatic pose*) I suppose he
mentioned a date. To meet the suits.

JACKIE: He said tomorrow afternoon.

AMANDA: Tomorrow after*noon*? You see? Typical! They expect you to drop everything and dash for the nearest airport. And then when you meet with them, they say they're also considering someone else for the part. And make you cool your heels for a day or two until you're so hungry for the job you'll give in to anything they say.... Could we take the picture, please.

JACKIE: I'm not happy with that pose.

AMANDA: Neither am I. It feels corny.

JACKIE: Maybe it would help if we ran through part of the scene.

AMANDA: Good idea.

JACKIE: Remember you're now in your old drawing room.

AMANDA: *(As she imagines the space)* I suppose he gave you the plane schedule and everything.

JACKIE: He even made the reservations.

AMANDA: What did you say to that?

ROY: Kenny, take it up one more notch.

JACKIE: I said we start rehearsal at noon tomorrow.

AMANDA: Exactly! Good for you! ...Cue me, Debbie.

DEBBIE: *(Getting her script)* I'm finding the place.

AMANDA: *(To* JACKIE*)* I suppose, if worse came to worse, I could fly out and back in one day. Miss one rehearsal, two at the most.

JACKIE: That's a tough trip.

AMANDA: Did he say when they planned to start shooting?

JACKIE: Next week.

AMANDA: Next *week*? Why that's totally impossible!
...Give me my cue, please, Debbie.

DEBBIE: *(Now on book; reading)* Pishchik says, "How
about the sale? Tell us what happened."

AMANDA: *(To* JACKIE*)* Of course, if I went out there,
I could tell them in person that I'm totally committed
for the next month or so.

JACKIE: Two months, really...

AMANDA: *(To* JACKIE*)* The point is, I'd insist they'd have
to work around me... Line again, Deb?

DEBBIE: "How about the sale? Tell us what happened."

AMANDA: And I suppose occasionally I could commute.

JACKIE: From Los Angeles to Buffalo?

ROY: You have to change in Chicago.

AMANDA: I could leave here after the Sunday matinee,
work there Mondays, and be back Tuesday evening.

DEBBIE: Would they allow that?

AMANDA: I'd demand it. I'd say the theater comes first.

DEBBIE: Which it should.

AMANDA: Besides it's only a recurring role. She comes
and goes.... Line, please, Debbie.

DEBBIE: "How about the sale? Tell us what happened?"

AMANDA: You'll be glad to hear I know this section.
(Acts it) "Is the cherry orchard sold?"

DEBBIE: Lopahin says, "Sold."

AMANDA: "Who bought it?"

DEBBIE: Lopahin says, "I bought it."

AMANDA: There are stage directions, aren't there?

JACKIE: *(Taking the script, reading)* Chekhov says, "Madame Ranevskaya is overcome. She would fall to the floor if it were not for the chair and table near which she stands..."

(AMANDA tries these directions.)

AMANDA: This feels terrible.

JACKIE: It looked terrible.

AMANDA: Let's do it again.. "Who bought it?"

DEBBIE: "I bought it."

(AMANDA does the prescribed business again. ROY's camera clicks away.)

JACKIE: Good.

AMANDA: I hated it.

JACKIE: It was fine.

AMANDA: I want to do it one more time. It felt false and fake. Now help me here, Jackie.... She wants to go to Paris, doesn't she?

JACKIE: Part of her does.

AMANDA: And she's got some money from a rich Aunt....

JACKIE: Very little money.

AMANDA: And now she's giving a party in her own home...

JACKIE: O K, Debbie. From the top.

DEBBIE: "How about the sale? Tell us what happened."

AMANDA: "Is the cherry orchard sold?"

DEBBIE: "Sold."

AMANDA: "Who bought it?"

DEBBIE: "I bought it."

AMANDA: *(Suddenly)* No, I bought it.

JACKIE: What?

AMANDA: Why not? Why doesn't she hold onto it herself? She has that money from that Aunt. She could take a second mortgage or something. And still go to Paris. Why does it have to be one thing or the other? Is that your Russian fatalism again? I mean, an American woman would want both. Help me out here, Jackie? What do you think?

JACKIE: I think you want to go to L A.

AMANDA: For a day or two, maybe.

JACKIE: Oh Amanda, what are you doing to me?

AMANDA: If I nail down that job, Jackie, I can come back and buy my grandmother's house! And fix everything up. And I'd bring my daughter here, away from all that crap in La-La land. And I'd come home all the time, and sit on the veranda with my grandson, so he can grow up with some sense of community in this wonderful old town. I mean, that's what the Lunts did, didn't they? They'd retreat to Wisconsin somewhere, to recharge their batteries. Same with me! Every season I'll do a play, Jackie. *The Seagull* and *Hedda Gabler*, and what's a good Shakespeare for me, Jackie?

JACKIE: *(Coldly; walking away) Much Ado About Nothing.*

AMANDA: Oh, Jackie. Don't get mad at me, please. I'll be back Wednesday. Or Thursday at the latest. I promise.

JACKIE: Get her a taxi to the airport, Roy.

ROY: Debbie...

(DAN comes on again.)

DAN: I'll drive her out.

AMANDA: Dan!

DAN: I chickened out. No follow through, once again. I just hung around and listened to you over the intercom in the waiting room.

ROY: That's called the Green Room.

DAN: See? Amateur to the end... *(To* AMANDA*)* Well, I can be your driver.

JACKIE: *(To* AMANDA*)* You're on the 7:15 to Chicago, and the 10:30 to L A. First Class, of course.

AMANDA: Thank God. So I can relax. *(To* DEBBIE*)* Flying First Class is one of the few good things about working in television, Debbie.

DAN: I'll ride out on the plane with you. Just to keep you company.

AMANDA: Sorry. I'll need my beauty sleep.

DAN: I'll at least get my car. *(He exits)*

AMANDA: I'll be back, Jackie.

JACKIE: Yeah, yeah.

AMANDA: Trust me. I'm a Buffalo Gal, remember? I don't back out of my commitments!

JACKIE: You'd better back out of that costume.

AMANDA: All right. And then I'll come say a very temporary goodbye. *(She goes.)*

JACKIE: *(Calling to the lighting booth)* Back to work lights, Kenny.

(The lights change.)

JACKIE: Roy, what time do the casting people close in New York?

ROY: Six- thirty, at the latest..

JACKIE: (*Checking her watch*) Jeffrey might still be there.
If not, call his cell. He should e-mail us a list of available
actresses immediately....

(ROY *goes.*)

DEBBIE: She said she'd come back.

JACKIE: The suits won't let her. At what they're paying,
they'll never buy this shuffle-off-to-Buffalo shit. Oh
she'll protest, of course. But they'll throw in limousine
service and a personal assistant. So she'll think about all
those lines she won't have to memorize, and the grungy
little dressing room she won't have to wait around in,
and those eight performances a week she won't have to
crank up for, and finally she'll agree to whatever they
ask....

DEBBIE: What about her contract?

JACKIE: Even if we had it in hand, we'd still have to let
her go. My God, if her series hits, she could make close
to a million a year for a possible seven years, plus even
more if it goes to syndication. How can we not let her
go? And what really pisses me off is that it might end
up being a good show.

DEBBIE: A television sit-com?

JACKIE: Some of our best young writers are out there
now, Debbie. Meanwhile, back at the ranch, we are
offering a measly six hundred and forty-six bucks
a week for seven weeks hard labor on one more
translation of an old Russian chestnut.... It would
be unconscionable to hold her.

DEBBIE: But she doesn't like it out there.

JACKIE: She likes paying her bills.

DEBBIE: You mean it all boils down to money?

JACKIE: Oh I think it's more than just money. It must be
cool to have people bowing and scraping all over the

world. In the theater you can rise to the top of your career, and barely get a nod from your doorman. Come Wednesday—no, make it Friday—after everyone in Hollywood has had a long, leisurely lunch, I'll get a tearful telephone call, followed by a gigantic spray of flowers for the Green Room. By then, we should have found someone to take her place.

DEBBIE: She wants to buy her grandmother's house.

JACKIE: She was improvising, Deb. That's what she does. Remember?

(JAMES *comes in.*)

JAMES: Ready for dinner.

JACKIE: Where's your lady?

JAMES: Meeting us at City Grill..

JACKIE: So's mine, I hope. *(Pause)* We've lost our star, Jim. To the world of television.

JAMES: It figures.

JACKIE: We'd lose you, too, wouldn't we?

JAMES: If I were a star.

JACKIE: Stars, stars, stars...

JAMES: The fault, dear Jackie, is not in our stars but in ourselves...

DEBBIE: That we are underlings.

JACKIE: Thank you, Debbie.... Are you still with us, James, even if our star is not?

JAMES: Jackie, baby, I'm an addict, remember. Once I'm in, you'd have to put me through de-tox to get me out.

(JACKIE *and* JAMES *embrace.*)

(DAN *comes back in.*)

DAN: Car's out front.

ROY: I'll check on our star. *(He exits.)*

JACKIE: *(To* DAN*)* Have you met James Johnson?

DAN: Oh! Hey! Wow! I saw you in *Two Trains Running!* You were fantastic!

JACKIE: *(To* JAMES*)* This is Doctor Rubin.

DAN: Robbins...I mean, Rubin. Oh hell, I don't know who I am.

JAMES: *(As they shake hands)* Try acting some time.

*(*ROY *comes back on.)*

ROY: She'll be right out.

DAN: Is it my fault? Did I scare her off?

JACKIE: She's scared of the stage.

ROY: And she's got a family to support

DEBBIE: We need government funding for theater in this country. Then this wouldn't happen.

JAMES:"''If a great many remedies are offered for some disease, it means it is incurable. I keep thinking and racking my brains. I have many remedies, ever so many. And that really means none...''

(Everyone looks at him.)

JAMES: That's from *The Cherry Orchard.* My character says it in the play.

*(*AMANDA *comes in. She is now dressed for travel and carries a small overnight bag.)*

AMANDA: Well I'm off.

DAN: Any more luggage?

AMANDA: Just this. *(Hands him her overnight bag)* Roy, I left my big suitcase in my dressing room. Would you see that it gets to my room at the Lenox?

DEBBIE: I'll take it over tomorrow.

AMANDA: Thank you, Debbie. *(Looking around)*
Well... What to say?

JAMES: "My sister! My sister!"

AMANDA: Oh yes! Exactly!... "My dear brother!"
(She kisses him) "...And my orchard—my dear, sweet,
beautiful orchard!" *(To* ROY*)* My life... *(To* DEBBIE*)*
My youth... *(To* JACKIE*)* My happiness... *(To all)*
Goodbye, goodbye..."

JACKIE: Christ, but you're good, Amanda!

AMANDA: I'll be better when I get back, I promise...
"One last look at these walls, at these windows...
My mother used to walk around this room..."

JACKIE: That's it!

AMANDA: Oh Jackie! This is what I came home for. This
dear old town, this special space, this sweet company,
these feelings I haven't felt for a long, long time....

ROY: Add a good audience, and we've made it a good
play.

JACKIE: Right. And remember that in Hollywood, this
whole scene would all end up on the cutting room floor.

AMANDA: I'll be thinking about all of you while I'm
there..

DAN: Will you be thinking about me?

AMANDA: When I'm not working on my lines.

DAN: (*to* DEBBIE*)* See? That's the sign of a real pro.

AMANDA: A real pro knows when to get off the stage.

*(*AMANDA *goes off.* DAN *remains for a moment)*

DAN: *(Quickly, to others)* I'll talk to her in the car. It's a
rare thing when you get a chance to change your life.

(AMANDA *comes on again*)

AMANDA: It's a rare thing in the theater when you ruin an actor's exit.

(AMANDA *drags* DAN *off.*)

(*Pause*)

JAMES: Things still on at City Grill, Jackie?

JACKIE: Too late to cancel.

JAMES: I'll call my lady.

JACKIE: (*Calling after him*) Reception's better in the Green Room.

(JAMES *goes.*)

JACKIE: O K, Roy. A few quick things, then we'll go be aggressively Chekhovian—and smile through our tears.

(ROY *picks up his laptop.*)

JACKIE: Adjust the schedule till we have her replacement.

ROY: (*Reading his laptop*) Teddy at Casting said Nancy Niles and Jennifer Michaels and Beverly Scott are technically available.

JACKIE: Try Jennifer Michaels first. They say she's weird, but worth it.

(ROY *starts to e-mail.*)

JACKIE: Roy?

ROY: Hmmm?

JACKIE: Why do you stay in this business?

ROY: I like all the talking.

JACKIE: Oh God. Talk, talk, talk. Onstage and off. It's all talk—and you like it?

ROY: I love it. I grew up in a kind of silence, remember. Both my parents were deaf as posts. So I've always gravitated toward the spoken word. *(As he works)* O K now I talk to my parents by signing, and I'll bet we communicate more than most families do. Maybe they can't hear but they sure know how to listen. Still I relish the sound of words. And I love the stage because we have this reverence for language. And any enterprise which depends so much on what people say, and how they say it, must be at the heart of what it means to be civilized. So I want to devote my life to it.

(DEBBIE comes back in, holding the necklace.)

DEBBIE: Look what Amanda left hanging by her mirror.

JACKIE: That chair still irritates the pants off me....

DEBBIE: *(Looking at necklace)* It's engraved. It says "Buffalo Gal".

JACKIE: I know what it says. ..I'll keep it for her, Debbie.

(DEBBIE hands JACKIE the necklace.)

ROY: The rest of the cast arrives on the nine thirty-eight Jet-Blue tomorrow morning. Ginny's offered her station wagon.

DEBBIE: I'll drive the van.

JACKIE: *(Moving the chair , looking at it)* That's better.... *(To ROY)* Remember to find out when Fiona breast-feeds. It might affect our rehearsal schedule.

ROY: *(Making notes)* Right... *(Checks his watch)* The Siegel's reservations are at six.

JACKIE: Why don't you start on over?

ROY: Come on, Debbie.

DEBBIE: *(To JACKIE, as she goes)* Sigmund Freud says that most plays end with a feast.

JACKIE: *(Calling after her)* Only if they're comedies, Debbie.

(ROY and DEBBIE go.)

(JACKIE sits alone, looking at the necklace.)

(A moment. Then AMANDA comes on.)

AMANDA: I forgot something.

JACKIE: *(Getting up)* You most certainly did.

(JACKIE hands AMANDA the necklace.)

(DAN comes on.)

(AMANDA looks at JACKIE, looks at DAN, looks at the necklace, as the lights fade on all three.)

(Curtain)

END OF PLAY